The Rattle Egg

poems by

Terri Witek

Finishing Line Press
Georgetown, Kentucky

The Rattle Egg

Publisher: Leah Huete de Maines
Editor: Christen Kincaid
Cover Art: Lucianna Chixaro Ramos
Interior Art: Terri Witek
Author Photo: Terri Witek
Cover Design: Elizabeth Maines McCleavy

Order online: www.finishinglinepress.com
also available on amazon.com

Author inquiries and mail orders:
Finishing Line Press
P. O. Box 1626
Georgetown, Kentucky 40324
U. S. A.

the rattle egg

X

4 F R

raiding

clarice

The carton arrives with 9 eggs. A purple country of symmetrical ups and downs. No lid. Or rather today's sky is a lid, differently blue. The eggs repose in their valleys. At ease, these sentinels. Who will soon be stolen the way things are always stolen, because they are elsewhere of use. Or (the word comes back) they may even desert. Where to? Some shore with its algae blooms? The beach does smell of eggs sometimes, or what we say to ourselves are "eggs." This open cardboard square, though, seems calm and simple: a terrain map of foundational impressions. Bottomed at the wide end of things. Which may be the sea again, blue-green tremblor and rising.

o o v o   é   ó b v i o

b   i

e

v   v

o   o o   o   o

▲

I haven't yet said this, out of timidity or disbelief, but one egg wears a little feather against its tan skin. Fluff at the bottom flattening to cling at the top, as if enacting in 2D the geometry of eggness. The feather tip's a bit crackish, or maybe more an inscription: forest leaf on wet ground. Who left what? We know a chicken casts eggs from its eden/idea in a trick of unplanned biology, but why did it cling? Or did the egg scrape then carry off a bit of the chicken's surface, its feathers not for flying, so that as the egg arrives at its place in the carton a chicken will have known momentary flight?

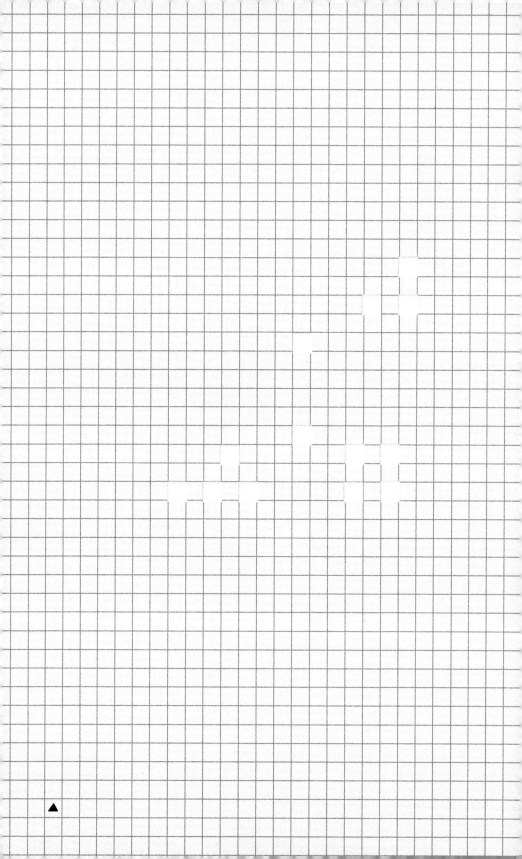

Of course it comes up: when the egg with feather is last in its box, should we eat it? We are practical people: we turn containers upside down to reach their last dregs. I am very loathe to eat the egg and my husband honors my aversion. I will eat chicken every night before I eat this egg.

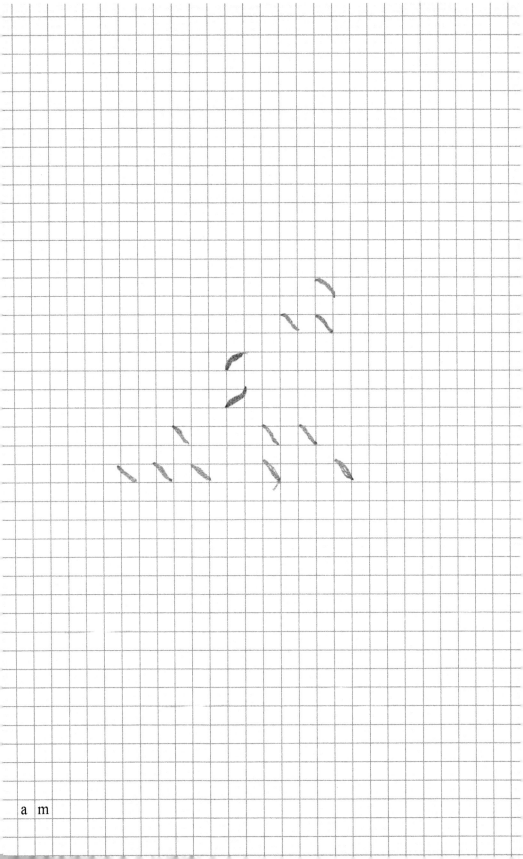

a m

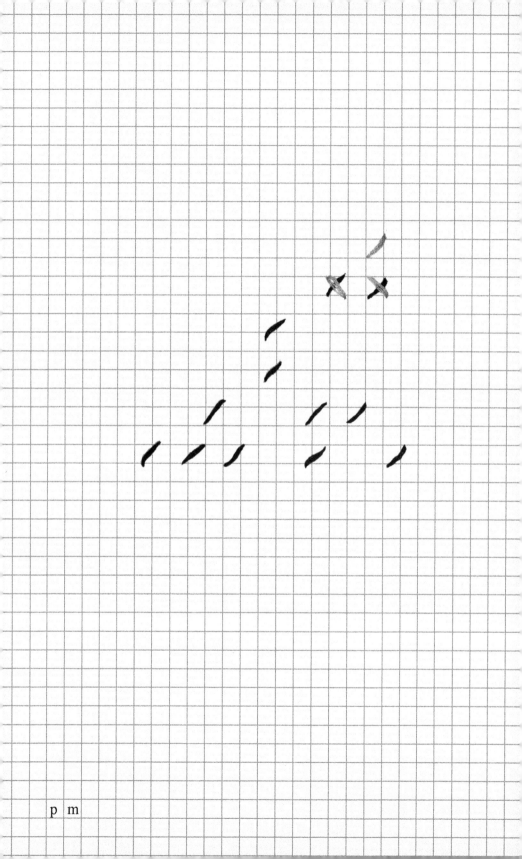

p | m

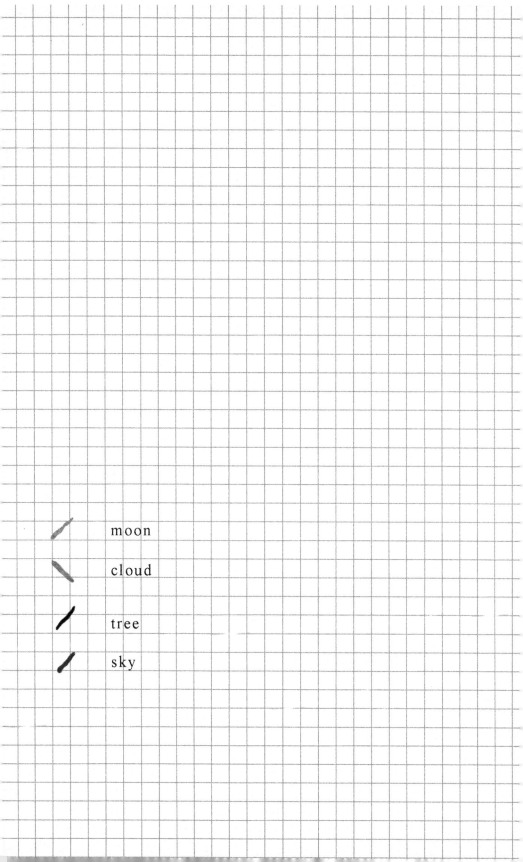

moon

cloud

tree

sky

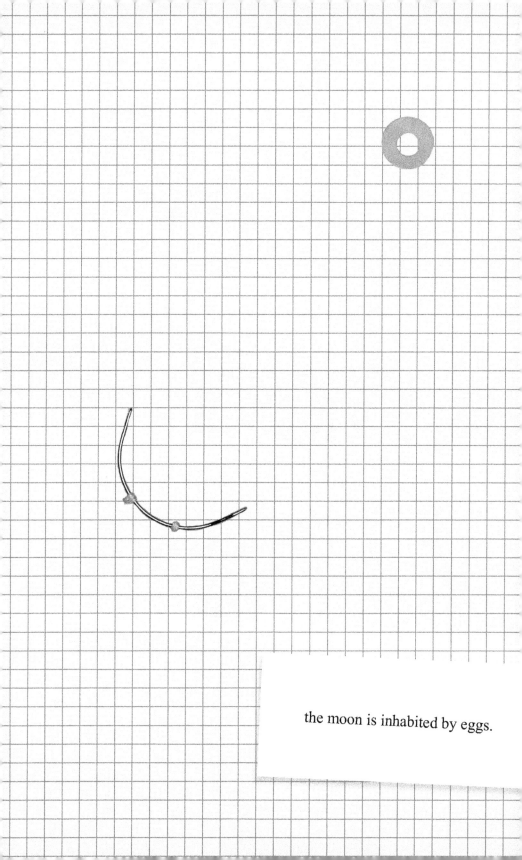

the moon is inhabited by eggs.

When I typed checken by mistake it seemed like any thought I hold next will require a procedure I have already missed. A check-in and maybe also a chick end---an examination not only of netherparts but of a life that never strictly happened. Confession: this is not a fertilized egg. I once knew an egg-handling place where they candled eggs to make sure. The square building was half-factory, with humming belts and clanking, but also strangely votive: small lights were banked in spots as if before absent statues. I gave the owner a nickel but that can't be right. Nor that I was sent here alone, though in retrospect I'm sure this too was practical: mother needed eggs so I walked to this dim, barnlike space inexplicably set into a hometown block. Webb-Gibeaux is what I remember: go to Webb-Gibeaux's and buy eggs.

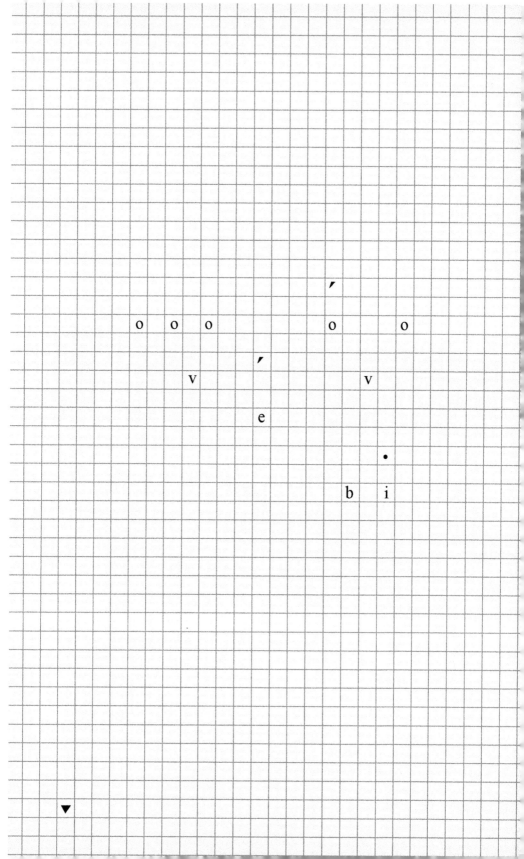

? = ▼

□ = ?

a possible way to read the legend:

/	street sign
o	manhole cover
v	corner
e	mailbox door
.	watermeter
b	wheeled trashcan
i	fire hydrant

Fortified by the sides of something, I ask worldwide Webb-Gibeaux how egg candling works. It's late: a sky factory of satellites already peers, block-by-block, further in. Spot your own prestige red dot? Who knew there were so many green grenade tree-bursts? But it strikes me again that I am not looking for childhood. That was fine but a little sad—half-fluff, half-inscription, with the stamp of banal origin. Collectable, of course. But I don't really care about that, or about an 11-year old with coins in her mitten who turned right from Lawrence Street onto Jefferson Street to buy eggs. This is not from lack of self-regard as I am in my own way a diva.

Some words I can stand to look at:

candling
red dot

Plus a wobbly stacker from wikiHow:

Look for signs that the **egg** is a winner.
Look for signs that the **egg** is a quitter.
Look for signs that the **egg** is a yolker.
If you are unsure, leave the **eggs** alone.

X

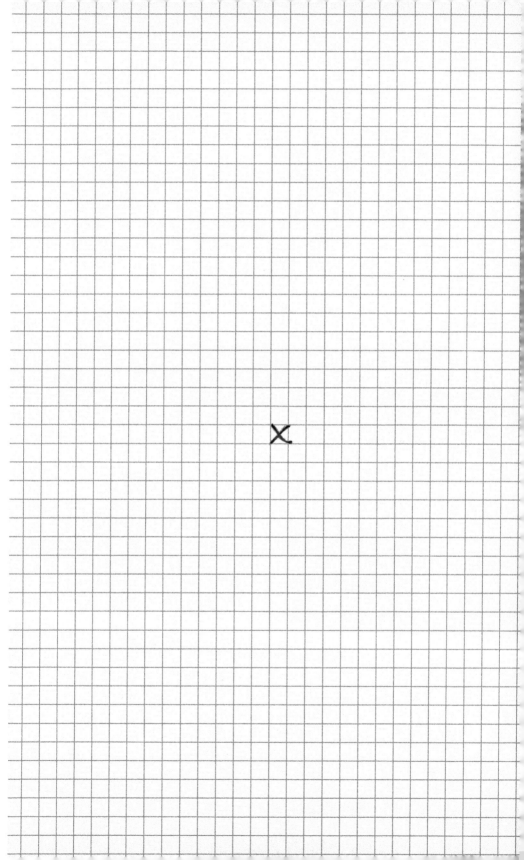

Admission: I can't help but wonder about eggs left behind. Post-menopause, do the remaining ones become little bubbles without a ride, become gods? Now, it seems, I'm only their cover story. Of course it's scientifically more precise to say they're unretrievable. 100,0000 pleasure in bed but if eggs escape this way, they evade both my lips and my peripheral vision. Eggs from the market, even swallowed whole, won't reach them.

Though today I saw a little broken one on the sidewalk, its yolk a smeared gold apostrophe. Didn't process the usual dismay because it's winter and—look up— there's no nest in sight. Maybe that joy-stab was only light through palmettos. Or wind ripple. Maybe the egg was a snake egg.

Yolk notes (a gema)

1.   Blastoderm   (see anagrams for blasto + skin)

öblāst f

1.   <u>district, region</u>
2.   <u>area, zone</u>
3.   <u>province</u>

bostal

1.   (Sussex) a small road leading up a hill. _{quotations ▼}

2.   Nucleus of pander   (**see center + pander**):
see also: **a third party**. An illicit or illegal offer, usually to tempt.

3.   Air cell (**see Anaximenes** _{quotations▼})

...... for since.....generated **in the flow of**......

egg count over time

Forgive me. Can't face the daily chart with its orangey-red graphics. To those accustomed to surveillance (say egg and a frying pan ad appears) the chart's merely clickbait, now's walk-in clinic. Though who ever objects to "the egg" translated to party favors? O hollowed-out sugar eggs bending little peep show tableaux. O greasy bright plastic whose beltlines crack open to candy. My eyes drift away. The egg has its own privacy laws, I suspect, so even if we glance in we can't really see it. Despite a quick flicker, like winter light reflected from mirror into room. We too have separated white from yolk, sliding egg-weight back and forth between half-shells. And we've all eaten that cake with its wave-whipped froth icing. Someone's breath at the candles.

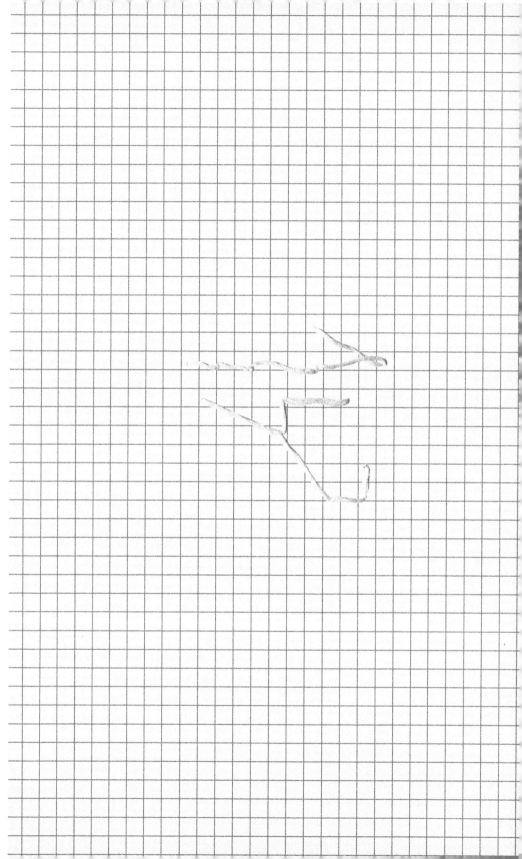

Some Field Notes

Number of O's in English text: 918
Number of V's in English text:166
Number of O's in English text: 918

?: If O = egg and V includes traces of chicken (see tooth; see nail), is the ratio of eggs to chickens (roughly 5.5 to 1 in English) an economically sustainable outcome?

?: Can this question be resolved by less granularity?

Words conjoining OV in English text and their x used:

love love love love love love love love love love love love love love love love love love
over over over
loves loves
cover
recovered
discovered
undercover
poverty
oval

Words conjoining VO in English text and their x used:
avoid avoid
devotion
volunteer
revolutionary

Does an egg in Portuguese leave trace that may be candled in English?

Words conjoining OVO in English text: 0

+ the indoctrination factor:

Egg Candler Operation Instruction:

1.   It's better in dark place or at night
2.   Just put the bigger side of egg to upsode
3.   Keep fire away
4.   Keep your sight away
5.   Intervaluse 10 ments

interlude + ibis =

Eggs with blowholes: our drowse-filled eyes. Winter light shifts eggs on the floor. What do we need from the market, my husband asks, typing. Everything I think of: tangerines, apples, brussels sprouts, can be handled less gently. The shapes will be suspicious, but I'll squint my peepers: stay fortessed.

O	love	error	for	to	something	from
ovo	for	proof	upon	could	destroy	of
look	do	error	love	rolled	once	from
one	know	not	you	for	of	not-
cannot	love	to	love	so	to	wanting
soon	of	about	you	long	recovered	whoever
becomes	would	about	doesn't	oval	one	to
ago	to	of	know	could	for	would
of	avoid	wonder	loves	no	to	losing
memory	removed	do	another	originated	one	own
of	from	know	do	Macedonia	whoever	therefore
only	only	of	not	of	for	our
one	one	almost	touch	most	topic	for
who	woh	do	of	arduous	over	body
one	world	therefore	do	spontaneit	not	body
too	would	know	not	y	once	proof
lost	world	don't	touch	of	adopted	does
promise	obvious	know	to	Macedonia	took	not
one	no	about	to	holding	one	do
thought	longer	don't	vision	foot	should	look
none	properly	know	of	so	one	to
looking	no	about	would	mother	topic	obvious
once	you	properly	to	for	becomes	cannot
no	you	Moon	to	constantly	to	about
does	to	exterior	world	too	discovering	cross
not	you	ization	yolk	of	of	loves
impossible	to	to	does	for	not	doesn't
supersonic	you	to	does	now	out	know
no one	to	into	no	revolut	to	would
does	nation	exposes	from	ionary	force	would
dog	not	whoever	wounds	to	to	lose
only	look	into	to	avoid	become	salvation
construct	not	whoever	from	cannot	not	for
ion	utmost	more	one	not	for	doesn't
shoulder	not	of	to	people	wouldn't	to
love	to	something	another	who	become	to
for	impossible	soul	one	those	our	so
cannot	to	of	God	people	grandiosity	does
	know	projectile	who	to	comes	looks
						not

know consists to chose no to love
or of however one longer another love
would bloody more who who from disillusion
no so important notice knows moment losing
would won't personal would of absolutely of
lose blood does good for person illusions
so looks not for so one people
doesn't horizon concern something attention those who
know from doesn't one to people would
so of recognize who forming who volunteer
only horizon does know would belong for
to coming recognize how of to love
undoing beyond outside to about Masonic love
comes mode something lose for society personal
born of impossible one now of on
to transport so who no those love
for for doesn't thought longer who poverty
found myopic recognize to about once love
not how look cover about to not
summoned could food precious don't protect moreover
out contra don't not only ones love
no diction recognize for broken who disillusion
comes of metamorp along on from of
sound one hosis one to destroying you
from originated not who to doing thought
unknown Macedonia to thought into so love
unknown most anymore to only consumed not
doesn't modern beyond not to only undercover doesn't
know of beyond formed one's among people
how pointlessly not one own sometimes love
to most now know for recognize no
know form no one those other to
error for longer one who love people
error to more those ones our who
don't found more words who though without
know on to on convent don't would
anymore nothing looked phone floor do personal
long to too to do though doesn't
to done long one without don't love
honest for to who glory longer honorable
only of who thought purpose love exception
our not to one-self job allowed those
vision to one who to to who
of of who those out more would
         so modesty

allowed
to
so
form
no
for
worse
other
people's
conditions
for
fo
also
without
our
so
form
upon
imposed
prone
to
arduous
committing
instruction
s
unsupport
ed
of
found
not
understoo
d
intolerable
could
no
longer
not
others
over
another
who
slowly
consumed
own

rebellion
rebellion
dicovered
two
or
instruction
s
no
explanatio
n
whatso
ever
another
too
thought
spoken
of
to
out
of
innocence
fool
harrdiness
loyalty
disloyal
those
of
job
cosmic
to
done
unfortunat
ely
cannot
into
consider
ration
those
who
become
insitutions
comprehen
sion
doesn't

motives
word
lost
shout
who
sprout
from
out
work
of
shouted
yolk
our
tolerable
not
most
of
freedoms
no
fool
most
to
point
wronging
others
so
job
to
purpose
most
job
into
one
money
allowance
to
so
form
money
for
other
purposes
bought
stock

modesty
to
also
so
honorable
form
for
completely
forgetting
or
to
to
so
mission
freedom
or
controlled
noticing
how
error
of
to
rebellion
for
nothing
of
one
second
to
absolute
love
money
to
of
nobody
knows
how
for
someone
whose
job
consists
of
who

own
whose
job
consists
of
forgetting
someone
of
whom
dishonor
not
mirror
or
of
righteous
know
doesn't
of
on
contrary
to
to
to
one
of
righteous
don't
how
attnetion
foolishness
could
out
through
properly
good
for
to
one
of
those
people
who
would
do
job

forget
notion
of
work
could
couldn't
to
out
on
own
work
out
to
longer
forever
to
other
to
also
worked
solely
for
something
not
know
instruction
s
for
once
know
not
recognizing
emotion
do
not
from
do
not
about
one
ploys
about
forgotten
protected

those
words
one
of
so
out
of
devotion
to
forgot
forgetting
forgetting
of
possessive
adoration
could
forgotten
only
of
forgetting
becomes
impossible
no
for
one
move
over
to
window
open
into
our
to
pallor

Though a friend claims all seeds are eggs. Ahh Cixous, in her own lavish carton. Showing up with pip-plump tangelos and so latterly with her insistence on the senses, the sentence, 5 ways in through the page-body. But the egg is already away. And so daily: clickcluck on a bootleg pdf faintly shadowed at one edge: an opening? A spine? Boom from the fortress: o ovo é ó b v i o.

a possible action at é:

Once I held 500,000 eggs but now the count is uncertain. I haven't bled for
____. If red were discovered on the __ now it wouldn't signal an egg escaping
its destiny but trouble further up in the factory. But just as when there's no
mail one day, a fat bundle leans by the wet door on the next, my body's excess
caution is matched by extravagance. I weep every few hours now, just as when,
8 years old, I could pee through my slip just by kneeling in a confessional box.
The grid slides open. A round light swells behind a shadow that's nearly solid,
that's voiced.

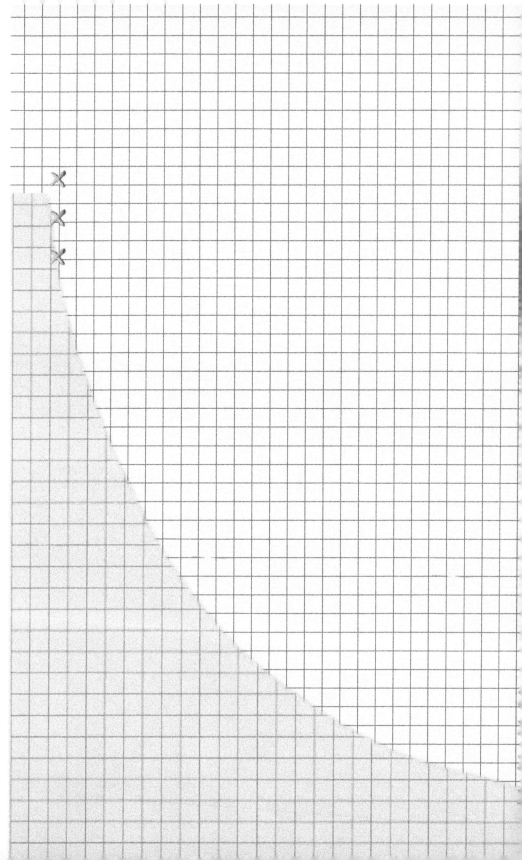

Which suggests that if we really consider the map, when isn't exactly a boundary. So I'm still at my 2nd Saturday job: scraping candle ends from little glass holders in church and inserting fresh candles for the next devotees. Fat white wax buttons. Soon change will clank through a metal mouth on the candle stand: this gives anyone the right to light up. Finished cleaning, I always do it myself. Performance piety: really I'd like to be first to re-burn. To leave wax I'll never see to its end. To bottom out. I poke at an x of metal anchoring each remainder and feel cloudy shavings under my nails—are fingernails my removal method? I must, after the first time, have carried a butter knife from home in my coat pocket.

Today, drinking coffee, I wonder about history: just when V first split first from its O. Oocyte— ootid—ovum: is this breakdown or progress? Yuri Herrara says change any front end and watch out. As he is Mexican with a Russian first name and has been confused online with a chanteuse famous for her song about pandas, Yuri helps me take heart. Steven Dunn helps too, saying he collects in his name both the father he never met as a child and a white poet whom people then compliment on the accuracy of his black voice. De-ovo it all. Protoovo it all. Little reyvolk (that walk).

Maybe, as egg gets closer to body, V is to foot as O is to face.   + this sidebar : according to the U of IL Extension, chicken feet diagram out like this:

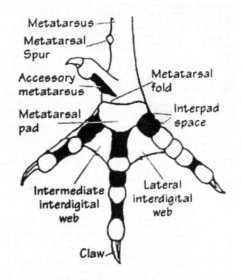

ovo	invisible	love	have
having	have	everything	have
eventually	obvious	vaguely	forever
indivisible	loves	several	ever
individually	save	advantages	have given
supervisible	survival	envy	everything
love	surviving	even	have
love	salvation	receive	given
love	living	even	every
avoid	living	very	privilege
alive	alive	received	devotion
obvious	even	revealed	self-serving
never	reverie	over	evasion
never	vision	leaving	never
having	given	even	living
gives	given	discovered	move
have	every	received	over
whoever	every	whatsoever	
love	believe	bravely	
love	cover	bravery	
even	have	naïve	
loves	give	everything	
vision	having	individual	
never	have	individuals	
invisible	convent	motives	
arrives	serving	various	
invisible	live	living	
have	live	living	
oval	never	liviung	
vessel	undercover	given	
vessel	love	mischievous	
traverse	love	given	
revolutionary	love	give	
lives	love	have	
avoid	volunteer	diverting	
haven't	love	having live	
recovered	love	every	
alive	lives	valuable	
whoever	love	love	
having	poverty	valuable	
over	love	give	
discovering	having	believing	
veracity	love	grave	
veracity	love	whatever	
verisimilar	vain	have have	
whoever	love		
advantage	exclusively		

pm again

I walk out with eggs: my irretrievable ones, and a hen's egg tucked down in my sports bra. Rattling in its little plastic carton as if my heart has come loose.

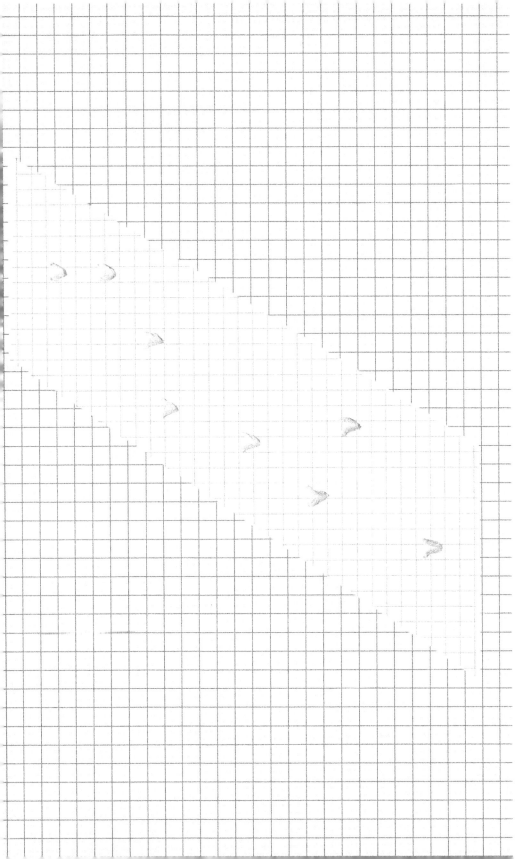

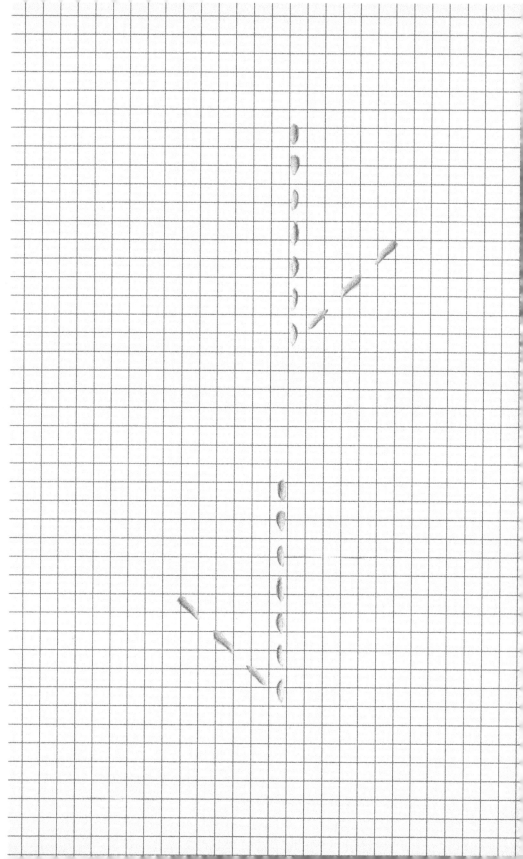

what happened at the corner
of voorhis and orange

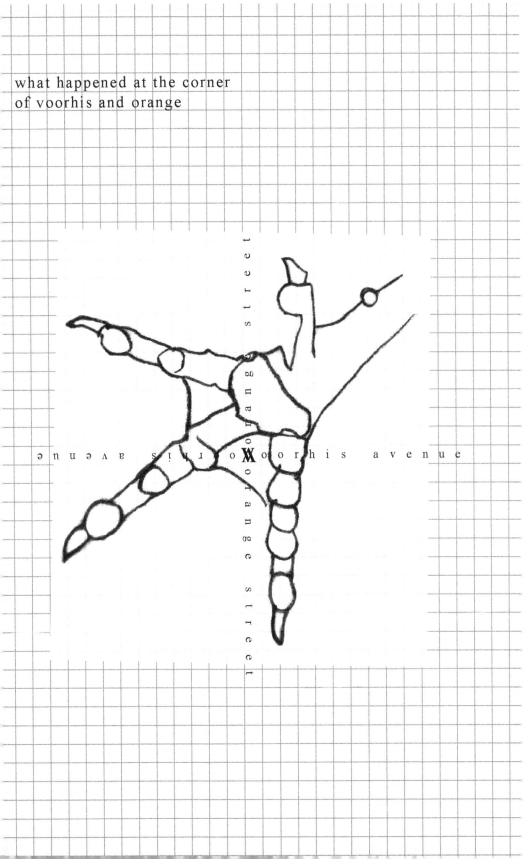

this corner was fenced:

am again

I tuck the egg into my hair and lie down on the pavement. The egg's been in the fridge too long now. I put a hand under my hair on the pavement to warm it. Maybe I'm not a holder of egg, but surround in turn surrounded. Maybe I'm an air cell or a nucleus of pander. Thin clouds blow sideways, a crazy pink. One wren then another. Owl. I am worried my husband will wake and, wondering where I've gone to, open our front door as clouds go gold. Optical out blocks away to my body, splayed with arms overhead. A little breeze feels like panic. Hurry, I say to the egg. Last chance.

000000000

Kk. I've ordered an egg candler, pretty sure I can't use it. But there's fast, free delivery, and I have the dosh. In the ad, a candler resembles a flashlight: choose a space age tip any hen can provide. But the FAQ's sell me, not the blunt, ugly image cinching flat background. Plus a battery pack for when the power goes. Plus the candler's mystery name, Magicfly, and its subtitle: Bright Cool LED Light Candling Lamp, whose bristling capitals a gaze can hardly cut a swath through.

Some things claimed in the FAQ's:

Long Electric Cable with American Plug
Suitable for school funny class
If you need the one with the battery, you can have this one: BOlLPXGZMM
You just can't tell before then

A big envelope appears: crinkly white, stickered with the driver's yellow ID: *tommy*. As usual I haven't heard a truck. The rectangle's sealed, nearly weightless. I lift it between my eyes and sky. Curiosity wins: I go in, cut open as always.

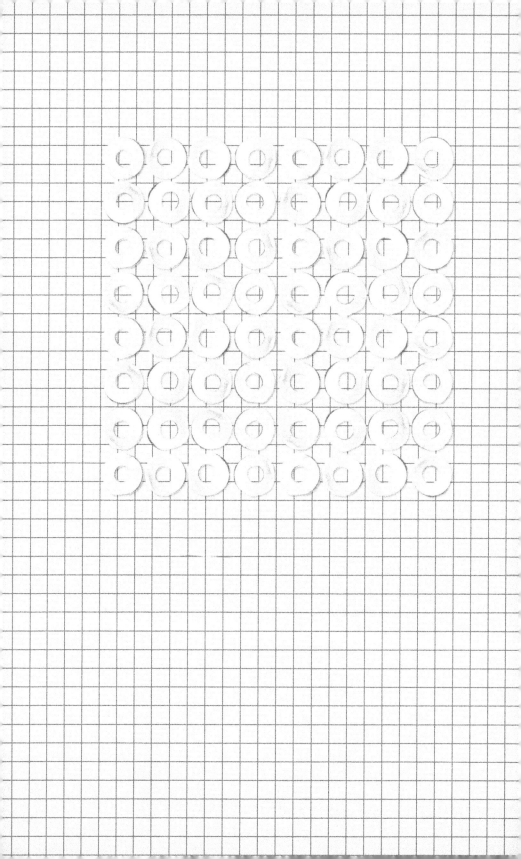

If you were to look back under my orders, a photo of this envelope appears, still tranquilly waiting. The house is yellow, clearly ours. The street sounds like cars passing. A dark door stays shut. No one would steal this envelope. Which looks like itself. Thin, strong. And, like sunlight at noon, perfectly empty.

I now think this envelope came from the egg.

To the egg:

I close one eye to you, feather-side out. You are indifferent, therefore easy. If snakes were eggs I could have bitten you. An egg in the hand is worth two in the foot. These selfies roll off so serenely I'm tempted to throw in the real deal: you, the genuine article. To bury you and grow chickenwire. To pitch you to the next hazy surfline as bubble. To watch as long as I can bear it until, grain by grain, purpling sands find and surround you, catch and build. You will be bright then. You will be so cool.

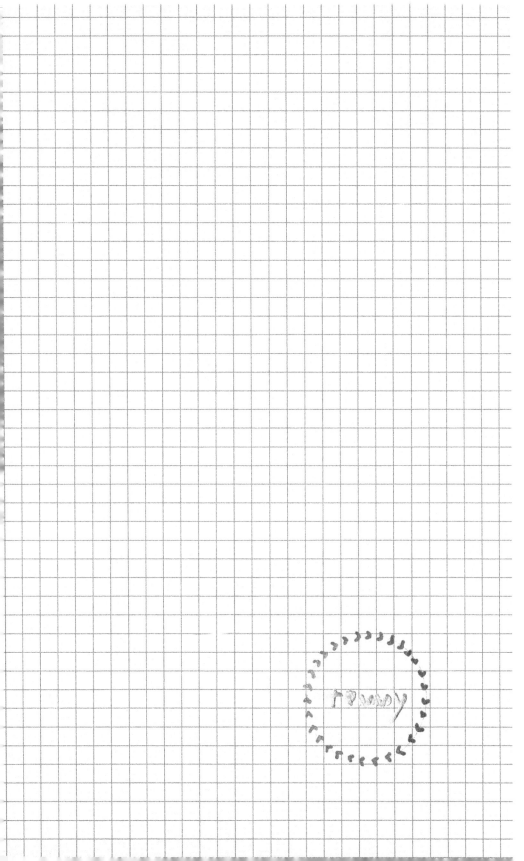

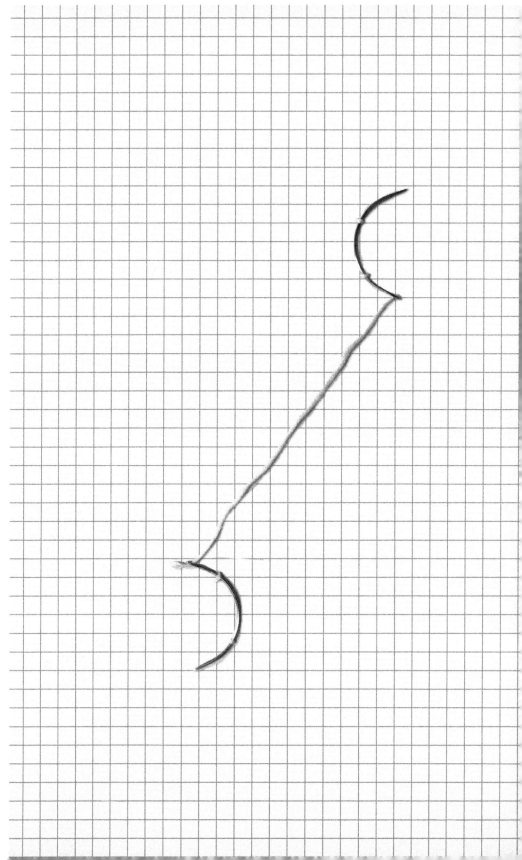

Notes and Acknowledgements

The Portuguese text of Clarice Lispector's "The Egg and the Chicken" begins with several o-filled paragraphs, a fact delightfully noted by Helene Cixous in Reading with Clarice Lispector.

The o's and v's tracked back though English in the Bills of Lading can be found in Katrina Dodson's translation of "O ovo e a galinha" in Complete Stories.

The maps of "o ovo é óbvio" were followed in Deland, Florida.

This project was partially funded by a Brown Innovation Center Inquiry Circle grant from Stetson University. Thanks to the interdisciplinary artists of Studio Circles E 1 + 2 : Madison Creech, Luca Molnar, Matt Roberts. Teresa Carmody, Katie Baczeski , Chaz Underriner, and Dengke Chen for their ideas and help.

Deepest appreciation to Lucianna Chixaro Ramos, who recreated *The Rattle Egg* for the page with her usual wit and care.

4FR thanks to Cyriaco Lopes for first sharing Clarice in Portuguese, and for the early collaborative translation of "O ovo ...e a galinha" which failed just enough to imprint it.

Poet **Terri Witek**'s sixth book of poems *The Rape Kit* is the Slope Editions Prize 2018 winner, judged by Dawn Lundy Martin. Martin calls *The Rape Kit* "a grand success, the best we'll get. Fresh, relevant, and heartbreaking" and "a fire in the throat of a culture that has no appropriate language for rape and its aftermath..."

Witek's poetry often traces the breakages between words and visual images. Her visual poetics work is featured in the 2021 anthologies *JUDITH* (Timglaset) and the *WAAVe Global Anthology of international visual poetry by women*. It has appeared in museum and gallery shows and in site-specific performances as well, often in collaboration with visual artists.

The poet's collaborations with Brazilian visual artist Cyriaco Lopes (cyriacolopes.com) have, since 2005, been shown nationally and internationally: in New York, Seoul, Miami, Lisbon, Valençia, and Rio de Janeiro. Since 2011, collaborations with new media artist Matt Roberts (mattroberts.com) often use augmented reality technology and have been featured in Matanza (Colombia), Lisbon, Glasgow, Vancouver, and Miami. Her new collaborative manuscript with poet Amaranth Borsuk loops the pandemic and the eco-crisis as a transmission of rain and smoke between worlds. Witek's individual poems have been featured in a wide variety of text venues, including *American Poetry Review, Poetry, Slate, Hudson Review, Lana Turner, The New Republic,* and many other journals and anthologies.

With Cyriaco Lopes, Witek team-teaches Poetry in the Expanded Field in Stetson University's low-residency MFA of the Americas; they also run The Fernando Pessoa Game as faculty in the Disquiet International Literary Program in Lisbon. Witek also directs Stetson's undergraduate creative writing program, and holds the university's Sullivan Chair in Creative Writing. terriwitek.com

CPSIA information can be obtained
at www.ICGtesting.com
Printed in the USA
LVHW011902241121
704185LV00005B/20